Poems

of

Inspiration

By

Ethel J. Hill

Introduction

I thank God for the gift that He has given me to write and be a vessel unto Him.

The poems in this book convey a variety of thoughts and beliefs: expressing love, hope, faith, and a bit of humor.

My poems are dedicated to my church; New Mt Zion Church of God Holiness, in Norfolk, Virginia. Worshipping there has increased my faith, and added immense joy to my life.

I am thankful for all of the sermons that I have heard, the lessons that I have learned, and the friendships I have known. Some of my poems are devoted to life and experiences that we may encounter from time to time. I have found that Christ is the answer for any problem we may have.

I believe that you will be inspired, in some way, as you read these God-given verses.

Oh let us magnify the Lord together!

CONTENTS

Your Life is a Book

Your life is a book, and it's being read
As you go along each day,
So watch the things you do
And be careful of what you say.

Whether you are weak or strong
Or have a daring look,
Remember my sisters and brothers
That your life is a book.

Whether your pages are thick or thin,
Someone can read them through.
The book may be dull or bright but
Someone is reading that too.

Your words may be many or few,
Spanish or English, you know,
Whether spoken in Greek or Latin,
Someone will tell you so.

If you are friendly or very shy,
Or ever so proud or bold,
Someone is reading you my friend
Whether you are young or old.

So be careful as you go along,
Be honest, and not a crook,
For wherever you go, whatever you do
Your life is a book.

Have Faith in God

"Have Faith in God"
was a sermon that I heard one night,
And my heart was really encouraged
For I knew the preacher was right.
Without faith it's impossible to please god,
And I believe it's true,
For it is written in God's word,
And that we should pursue.

By faith Moses went to Egypt land
As God gave him command.
He knew that he was protected
By God's powerful hand.
The just must live by faith,
And that we must believe,
For we walk by faith and not by sight,
A blessing we receive.

By faith old Noah built the ark
And the people laughed at him.
But when the rain began to fall,
Noah could have laughed at them.
With God all things are possible
And He won't ever fail.
Faith is the victory, I'm told
And it will help when foes assail.

So let's stand for God's Word and obey it,
Not matter what others do.
Stand and never doubt Him
And He will stand for you.

That sermon truly encouraged me
To continue to take a stand,
And I know the Lord will stand by me
If I obey his command.

It's Good to Have Friends

It's good to have friends
That's very true
And you can go to them
When you are feeling blue.
Friends are people that you can trust
And they can trust you too.
They know your ups and downs
But they won't tell on you.

Very good friends are hard to find
But you can find them if you try.
When you do find true friends
They won't ever pass you by.
You'll have to show yourself friendly
If you want to get a friend,
And you will find a few good people
On whom you can depend.

I'm glad that I have good friends
And they've never let me down...
If I need them morning, noon, or night
They never seem to frown.
Where ever I go, I find a friend
And I am their friend too.
So I'll continue to find good friends
As onward I pursue.

How Can You Sleep at a Time Like This?

Just look all around you at the happenings of the day,
How people seem to want things to go in their own way.
If you stand up for the right thing, people will look at you and
hiss.
I don't see how anyone can sleep at a time like this.

There is a famine in the land for the gospel,
And the Bible said this would be.
False preachers are destroying the people,
And I'm sure that you'll agree

.

Most of them are out just for the money,
And they are not concerned about man's soul
They ride around in their big expensive cars,
Wearing designers' suits and fine gold

Some of their lives are so dirty,
You dare not greet them with a kiss.
Now tell me sisters and brothers,
How can you sleep at a time like this?

The divorce rate is going higher and higher,
The crime wave is rising too.
Children are disobedient to their parents,
And you know that this is true.

A house that is divided
Cannot stand, and the Bible does declare,
We must believe God's Word
Just like it is written there.

When Satan tries to tempt you,
Send him away with a whisk.
Quickly let him know that you are not
Sleeping at a time like this.

Don't Worry

When your day is dark and dreary,
And you don't know what to do,
Lift your head, please don't worry,
Jesus Christ will take you through.

No matter what your problems are,
Whether they are great or small,
Jesus is near, He isn't far,
He will help you bear them all.

If your health seems to be failing
Or you may be suffering in pain,
Jesus, our friend, will not forsake you,
He understands your losses or gains.

So don't be weary in well-doing,
Strive to always do what's right.
You'll be blessed as you go forward
Daily walking in His Light.

Don't be weary, just keep hoping,
Trusting faithfully in the King.
He has promised to defend you
If on you He can depend.

Though all earthly friends forsake you,
Just remember, His Word is true.
Don't be weary, He'll be right there
Until your journey here is through.

<u>Wait on the Lord</u>

Wait on the Lord in all that you do
Have faith that He will see you through
Trials big and trials small,
He'll give you strength to bear them all.
Wait on the Lord, each passing day,
Believe His Word and humbly pray.
He'll give you grace and power too
Wait on the Lord, He waits on you.

Whenever your ways is dark or dim.
Just keep the faith and trust in Him.
Hold to His hand, you will prevail,
Wait on the Lord, He never fails.
He promised to supply your needs,
If to his Word, you will take heed.
So cling to him and stand for right,
Wait on the Lord, His is the Light.

Good things will come to those who wait,
So just believe, He won't be late.
He'll come on time and answer you,
Just wait on him, His Word is true.
Whatever betides, don't lose your aim,
But everywhere, His Word proclaim,
And cast on Him your every care.
If you are weak, ask Him for strength,

For in Him are no depths or lengths,
He'll heal your soul and body too.
I know He will your strength renew.
The darkest night, or the brightest day,
he'll lead you safely in the way.
So keep your hearts on one accord,
And wait, I say, upon the Lord.

LIFE

It's often been said "Life is what you make it."
It's surely a struggle from birth to the grave.
There are some things that we really need,
Then there are other things that we crave.

Some take life for granted
And just throw it away.
I know it is a blessing,
And I value it each day.

Some folks are selfish,
Seeking only money and pleasure
But life doesn't consist
Of the abundance that we treasure.

Life with peace is beautiful,
When we truly love from the heart.
If it's live through strife and vainglory,
We need to make a brand new start.

Love should be the center of all of our lives,
We should be patient and true.
What good is your life full of misery,
When you don't know what to do?

Yes, live your life to the fullest.
Don't forget the One who gave it.
Ask Him to keep you in control,
For He's the only One that can save it.

<u>One Morning</u>

When I awoke one morning,
And began to look around,
I said "Thank you, Jesus"
For sending the Spirit down.

I thanked Him most of all for life,
And for watching over me
Through dangers, seen and unseen,
And keeping me filled with glee.

I thanked Him for legs to let me walk
And for eyes that I might see,
I thanked Him for ears to hear
His truth that makes me free.

I had a headache that morning,
And terrible pains in my chest;
But I was thankful to be living,
To be among the blest

I was neither hungry nor homeless,
And wondering where to go,
For the Lord prepared a way for me
That's why I love him so.

Jealousy

Jealousy is a terrible thing
We know that this is true.
It will make you get to the place
That you won't know what to do.

Jealousy has broken up many a home,
And I'm sure that you'll agree.
Somebody told a jealous lie
About something he didn't even see.

Jealousy will make you hate
Even your closest friend.
When she is doing all she can
To try to help you win.

Jealousy will make you envy
Your brother's car or home.
No matter how he got it,
Why should you sit and moan?

Some folks have children who are tall and thin
While others may be fat.
At times the devil will fill your heart
To even be jealous about that.

Don't be jealous if a man
Treats his wife and family nice.
Just treat yours in the way that you ought.
Will you take that advice?

11

If a brother teaches a lesson
And the Spirit uses him.
Don't you be so jealous
That you try to condemn.

If a brother picks a sister up
Maybe once or twice,
Sometimes you'll not be satisfied,
Until you tell his jealous wife.

If you see a man and woman talking,
Though it means nothing at all.
Someone with a jealous spirit
Will try to make them fall.

We all know that God is jealous,
And that we can't condemn.
He wants us to serve Him wholeheartedly
And put our trust in Him.

Now, friends, please listen to me
Don't let jealousy bring you down.
For if that one action controls your life,
It will make you lose your crown.

Prayer Time

Heavenly Father, in Jesus' Name,
I humbly come to Thee,
Thanking you for everything
That you have done for me.

I thank You most of all for life,
And letting me move about,
I thank You for Your precious Word
And It, I will not doubt.

I thank You for the mercy,
You've shown to me today,
And for Your loving kindness,
That's why to Thee I pray.

Please guide my mind to think right,
And for you I will speak,
Help me to shun all evil,
And strengthen me where I'm weak.

Lord, I know that without You
I couldn't even live,
And that's why I'm so thankful,
And to You my life I give.

You understand my broken English,
For Thy Spirit on me You do send,
Please give me love for everyone,
This is my prayer, Dear God.
Amen.

November 20th at Zion
November 20, 1966

"Humble Yourselves" was the subject
Preached by Preacher McNeal.
If you have a humble spirit,
You'll know your faith is real.

God will exhort you in due time,
So don't be in such a hurry.
Be humble and keep yourself in line,
Then you don't have to worry.

God's word means just what it says
So be submissive to Him.
His thoughts are higher than yours,
And that we can't condemn.

Through Christ we can do all things
And He won't ever fail.
A humble mind will bring you peace
If you let him prevail.

Jesus was obedient and humble
Even unto the death of the cross,
And God exalted Him above others.
Now, without Him, we are lost.

Every knee shall bow before Him.
For He has charge over earth and heaven,
And without a humble spirit,
Satan will keep us on his level.

Mt. Zion; First Day of May

The service at Mt. Zion was wonderful on the first day of May,
Beginning with Sunday School, and I'm proud to say
We had seventy-five souls in class that day.
It made the service come alive, in a special sort of way.

The lesson was about Ahab,
And his wife Jezebel,
The scheme she used
To have Naboth killed.

In I Kings, the second chapter will tell,
But God sent a prophet and he foretold their fate.
We know they both did meet their doom
But I don't know the date.

It doesn't pay to covet,
Not even your neighbors wife,
Just be pleased with what you have,
For you might lose your life.

If you want a new home,
Just get out there and work.
Please don't covet your neighbor's house
And sit around and shirk.

You will find out if you covet,
Said the pastor on May first
You are only hoping the other fellow
Will come out with the worst.

So let's covet or desire spiritual gifts,
And try to wear a smile,
Then we won't let old Satan
Within our hearts beguile.

For "the lack of knowledge",
the pastor quoted
Hosea 4:6
If you read the entire chapter
The people were in a fix

We need to know the word of God,
Not going by what we hear
Sit down, take time to read
The Bible, the end is near.

People are really being destroyed
Because they are rejecting the word of God.
Though God has promised to punish them
Right here on the earth they trod.

Oh Joy! God gave to us one soul that night
And we all were very proud.
It made our hearts rejoice because
He came out from the crowd.

We came to the Lord with boldness,
And shook the pastor's hand
And he declared to the church of God,
That for it he would stand.

The Lord was surely in our midst
He sent some visitors by
One of them was a very dear soul
Who had once played for the choir.
So let us never ever forget
The service on the first day of May
For God surely poured out His blessing
In Mt. Zion on that day.

First Thessalonians, Fifth Chapter

But of the times and seasons,
I have no need to write,
For you all know perfectly
The Lord will come as a thief in the night
When we shall say peace and safety,
Destruction will suddenly come,
Don't let darkness overtake you,
And the Lord find you undone.

Ye are the children of the light,
And the children of the day,
So let's not sleep, as others do,
But watch, be sober, and pray.
Put on the breastplate of faith and love,
And the helmet of salvation,
For God has not appointed to wrath,
So be a light for the nation.

Christ died that we should live together,
Whether we are awake or sleep,
To edify one another with comfort,
And His Word He wants us to keep.
Know the ones which labor among you
In the Lord, and esteem them high,
In love for their work's sake,
Have peace, don't just pass them by.

Warn them who are unruly,
Comfort and support the weak.
Be patient toward all men,
But never any evil seek.
Follow that which is good,
Among yourselves and all men.
Pray without ceasing, rejoice evermore,
And give thanks unto the end.

This is the will of God concerning you,
In Jesus Christ I say,
Quench not the Holy Spirit,

BROTHERHOOD

Brotherhood isn't just a word
It's something to be shown
By helping one another
And not casting stone for stone.
The color of the skin doesn't matter,
Or whether he's short or tall,
Remember that's your brother
Whether he's great or small.

Brotherhood can be proved
By helping others to win,
Even if he's your enemy,
Prove to be his friend
We all came from Adam and Eve,
No matter what others say,
God made the woman from Adam's rib
That's why we have brotherhood today.

I believe that God honors brothers
Who will work together in love,
And will speak out for Him boldly,
Yet are as harmless as a dove,
So, men, keep brotherhood in action
And strive to do your part,
By esteeming others higher than yourself
With a meek and humble heart.

It's Up to You

It's up to you to smile
It's up to you to frown
It's up to you to cry
Or run around the town

It's up to you to stand up
It's up to you to fall
It's up to you to be firm
Or answer to the wrong call.

It's up to you to be happy
It's up to you to be sad
It's up to you to do good
And make someone else glad.

It's up to you to walk
It's up to you to ride
It's up to you to stay in the light
Or find a place to hide.

It's up to you to work
It's up to you to steal
It's up to you to shirk
Or beg for every meal.

It's up to you to be strong
It's up to you to be weak
It's up to you to be bold
Or slip around and sneak.

It's up to you to give
It's up to you to keep
It's up to you to laugh
It's up to you to weep.

It's up to you to read
It's up to you to write
It's up to you to play
It's up to you to recite

It's up to you to be kind
It's up to you to be true
It's up to you to obey
Or be stubborn as you pursue.

It's up to you to learn
It's up to you to teach
It's up to you to get wisdom
If you someday want to preach.

No one can make you do
Anything that you don't want to do.
Whatever you make of yourself in life
Is strictly up to you.

My All in All

My all in all is Jesus
And I am very glad
For He is the dearest Friend
That I have ever had.

No matter what I tell Him
Whether it's great or small
He never tells another
Though I rise or fall.

If I make an error
He understands my aim.
He shows to me His mercy
That's why His Work I'll proclaim.

He sees me everywhere I go
And guides me on my way.
He gently whispers peace to me
And watches over me night and day.

My All in All is Jesus
He saved my soul from sin.
When I came to Him believing His Word
He sweetly took me in.

He's never left or forsaken me
And I know that He loves me too.
I can see His blessed favor
In all that I attempt to do.

My All in All is Jesus
I can cast on Him my cares.
For He is always willing
To listen to my prayers.

He heals me when I'm sick
And lets me rise and go.
That's why I love Him so much
And I want the world to know.

My All in All is Jesus
And I will praise His name
Through trials and tribulations
For He's always the same.
Whatever I need, He will supply,
For He owns everything.
That's why I keep my trust in Him
And to Him I will always cling.

He gave His life for me one day
And I am very proud
So then I gave my Life to Him
And left the worldly crowd.

I can always depend on Jesus
For He hears me when I call
And I will firmly stand for Him
For He's my All in All.

My Little Girl And Boy

I

There's something that's a part of me
That really gives me joy,
I'll tell you what that something is,
It's my little girl and boy.

II

Although sometimes they fuss and fight,
Like any sister and brother,
But that's alright, I know they wouldn't
Take anything for each other.

III

When my little girl goes to the store
To buy some cookies and candy,
My little boy holds out his hand
And she thinks he's a dandy.

IV

Sometimes when their dad comes home,
I've really been annoyed,
They meet him on the step sometimes,
But I act as though I've been enjoyed.

V

You should see them all around their dad,
And he takes them in his arms,
And Oh! The noise they make sometimes
Is like sounding an alarm.

VI

I read the Bible to them at times
And then sometimes we pray,
For I don't want my boy and girl
To ever go astray.

VII

When I put them to bed sometimes
They want a very long talk,
And while I'm teaching my boy his prayers,
My little girl begins to walk.

VIII

Every Sunday morning
We prepare for Sunday School,
But I don't wait until Sunday
To teach them the Golden Rule.

IX

Sometimes when I am feeling bad,
They ask me how I feel,
They tell me that they love me
And that gives me a thrill.

X

They might not be so famous
Nor ever appear as a star,
But that's alright, I love them
Just the way they are.

XI

Some people don't like children
But my two bring me joy,
Charlette and Michael Anthony,
Are my girl and boy!

Why Do You Go to Church?

Why do you go to church?
Can you answer that right away?
Or do you need some time to think,
Perhaps a night or day?
Do you go to receive strength for your soul,
Or just to sit and see
The faults that are in your friends,
Your sisters and brothers, or me?

Why do you go to church?
Just to show an expensive dress,
And to say that the clothes that others wear
Seem to cost much less?
Do you go to get in a certain group
To talk about the preacher,
The deacons, ushers, organists,
And the Sunday School teacher?

Why do you go to church?
Just to see who shakes each other's hand,
Or to eavesdrop on a conversation,
Instead of listening to God's plan?
Do you go to church
Just to have somewhere to go,
So that you can tell your neighbors
All the church business that you know?

You should go to church with a spiritual purpose in mind;
To receive a blessing for your soul.
You should keep your conscience clear
By letting the Savior take control.
So think the question over
That I've asked in this little rhyme,
For if you don't go to church for a good reason,
You are only wasting your time.

SELF EXAMINATION

I was sitting around one morning
Thinking about myself,
So I took a paper from off the desk,
And a pencil from the shelf.

I told myself, "Joe, You're undone."
And it sort of bothered me,
Then I continued to examine myself,
For there was a lot I could see.

I had found myself complaining
When I should have been giving praise
Thanking God for his mercy,
And for keeping me all of these days.

Within myself I felt ashamed
So I sat and dropped my head,
And asked the Lord to forgive me
For the wrongs that I had done or said.

I often give myself an examination
For I can't exam you,
I have to give an account of my deeds,
Not what others do.

So give yourself an examination
To see how it will be,
If you find yourself undone,
Then confess it, just like me.

ONE WEDNESDAY EVENING

I

One Wednesday evening
I was on the front,
The children were playing
And doing a stunt.
The name of the stunt
Was called "Giant Step",
Those children surely had
A lot of pep.

II

I looked across the street
The neighbors were out
Some had a smile,
Others had a pout.
Some of them were coming
Home from work
Some were cutting grass,
Others were digging dirt.

III

The lady next door
Was picking her toes,
My boy came to me
With a running nose.
I looked up the street
A car came by:
An airplane then made
A noise in the sky.

IV

I looked down the street
A little girl had a ball,
Soon after that,
The little boy had a fall.
I called my little girl
And sent her to the store
To get Kool-Aid and cookies
For three or four.

V

I took my folding table
And put it on the ground.
And you should have seen
Those children gather around.
They ate and drank
With a lot of yak
And I really think
They enjoyed that snack.

If Jesus Came to My House

I

If Jesus came to my house,
To spend some time with me,
I'd be the happiest person
That ever you did see.

I'd gladly meet Him at the door,
And clasp His hand in mine,
For I would be so happy
To have a friend so fine.

II

I'd let Him sit in the finest chair
And in the finest place.
I'd make Him very comfortable,
As I'd look upon His face.

We would have a good conversation
About our love for each other,
For I'd be very happy to see Him,
For he's closer than a brother.

III

I wouldn't have to hide a comic book,
Or keep the neighbors out,
For the life I live before them
Would be worth talking about.

I wouldn't have to dust the Bible
Before reading a verse or two,
For I read it very often,
And that's what we all should do.

IV

I wouldn't worry about a car
To take Him anywhere,
First I would manage to make things nice for Him,
He'd be pleased to stay right there.

If Jesus should get hungry
I'd see to it that He got fed,
And if He got sleepy,
I'd give Him the finest bed.

V

If Jesus came to my house,
I'm sure it would be a joy.
I believe that He would talk
To my little girl and boy.

He'd tell them how much He loves them
And how they should love Him too,
And how they should acknowledge Him
In all they say or do.

The Tragedy of the Challenger

McAuliffe, Smith, Scobie, Resnick
Jarvis, McNair and Onizuka
These are the names
Of the seven astronauts that went up in flames

When they boarded the Challenger
Little did they know
That the space shuttle
Soon would explode

I saw the smoke and flames in the sky
I said to myself, "Oh, Lord, they'll all die."
My heart was saddened by the tragedy
For that was an awful sight to see

One teacher, flight commander, pilot,
Two electrical engineers,
A physicist and an aerospace engineer
Whom their families loved so dear.

When the Challenger exploded
These astronauts didn't have a chance
It left their families, friends and the nation
Almost in a trance.

There were fathers, mothers, sisters and brothers
Who met their terrible fate
I pray that God will comfort the families
But they will never forget that date.

"Obviously a major malfunction"
From the control room these words were spoken
Then a few seconds later
Many hearts were broken

"The Challenger has exploded"
Were the words from Nesbitt's voice
Someone had to break the news
And I don't think he had a choice.

In time the Lord will mend the broken hearts
For he understands just how they feel
And earth has no sorrow
That heaven cannot heal.

*This commemorative poem was composed on February 6, 1986 and is dedicated to the memory of the Challenger crew.

Where Are You Going?

Where are you going, and when will you stop?
Will you keep on going or get discouraged and flop?
Do you know the way, or are you trying to find
A place that will give you a peaceful mind?

Did someone tell you about a certain place,
Or are you just going on just to be in a race?
Is your mind made up to go all the way,
Or will you let some obstacle make you stray?

Is the place that you are headed for bright and fair,
And will you find more pleasure there?
Where are you going? Do you really know?
Will you go in a hurry, or will you go slow?

If you go too fast and have a breakdown,
Will someone else obtain the crown?
Where are you going, below or above,
And will the place be filled with love?

If I decided to follow you,
Would you gladly take me there too?
Will the rich be there, or only the poor?
Or can just anyone enter into the door?

Suppose I was ragged or my clothes were a mess,
Would I have to wear a certain kind of dress?
Would I need any money to buy things, or so
Or is everything free at that place that you go?

Will it be a place where the saints can dwell?
Or would you prefer not to tell?
Unless you tell me, I have no way of knowing
So please answer and tell me,

Where are you going?

One Tuesday Night at Old Mt. Zion

"Stand" was the text on Tuesday night
Preached by the minister with zeal.
He expounded to the Word of God,
And our hearts with spirit were filled.

His text was taken from I Corinthians 15:57,
And he surely preached with the power
That was given to him from heaven
In that wonderful hour.

Be steadfast and unmovable,
The preacher said that night,
Resist the devil and he will flee,
And in His Word remain.

If all of your friends forsake you,
And scandalize your name,
Stand up for the Lord with boldness
And praise Him, just the same.

No matter what the problem is,
Stand, and don't be shaken,
The Lord is watching over you,
He knows the way you've taken.

Give thanks to God for the victory
He gave to us through His Son.
Work for Him and serve Him
Until your day is done.

You won't have to worry about your pay,
For he will pay you right,
He'll give to you eternal life
If you believe Him and stand for right.

Just Stand on the Corner

Just stand on the corner, if you want to see a show,
And watch all the people go to and fro.
Some of them are clean and look very nice,
Others look as if they need some good advice.

Some of them have smiles on their faces,
Others are talking about certain unholy places.
Some are dark, and some are fair.
Others need to comb their hair.

Some are decked out in fancy dress,
Then some others look quite a mess.
Just stand on the corner, and you will hear
Some words that are spoken loud and clear;

Some sound good, and some sort of bad;
Some are spoken cheerfully, while others are sad.
Just stand on the corner all by yourself,
You will hear what your neighbor has on the shelf.

If she bought a dress, whether it's used or new;
Just stand around and you'll hear that too.
If the furniture is mahogany, or just oak wood;
You hear that she bought it, just because she could.

Did you ever stand on the corner in morning
And hear that other people are admiring

Whether the dress is short or long,
Or whether the person is weak or strong?
You'll hear about what the jewelry cost,
And whether it was found or lost.

Just stand on the corner
You'll hear about children too;
What they have to say,
And what they try to do.

Whether they sit around and pout,
Or have become high school drop-outs.

Just stand on the corner
If you want to hear about the preacher,
The deacons, ushers,
And the Sunday School teacher.

Now the corner is not the only place
That you can see or hear things of disgrace.
For people are talking everywhere
About the happenings here and there.

So when you are on the corner,
Be sure that you are not the one
Who has done the talking
When day is done

I Know

I know the Lord is with me,
For He never lets me down.
I can feel His presence,
Though sometimes I frown.

I never shall forget Him
He has done so much for me,
He even gave His life,
That from sin I could be free.

I know He watches over me
Every night and day.
At times when things seem gloomy,
He always makes a way.

Sometimes if I am burdened,
I think of how He cares,
I am glad that He is able
To all my burdens share.

I know the Lord has promised
A crown for righteousness,
If I believe and obey His Word
I'll be numbered among the blessed.

I know He sees and hears me,
Whatever I do or say.
I know that He will keep me
In His holy way.

I know He sends the sunshine,
I know He sends the rain,
He has no respect of person
On whom to send the golden grain.

I know the Word of God is true,
It was given from above,
It was written by the men of God,
Whose hearts were filled with love.

I know the Lord will save you
And will give you a peaceful mind.
He'll take away that stony heart,
And give you one that's kind.

So just believe the Word of God,
Though your steps are growing slow,
Take Him at His precious Word
He'll bring you out, I know

<u>Advice To Parents</u>

Parents, if you don't like the teacher,
Please don't let the child know it
For when that child faces him or her,
In some way, they will show it.

Please teach your child to always
Obey and respect the teachers,
For a teacher, too, can tell them right,
Although they are not preachers.

If my children tell me
The teacher punished them or so
All I ever say to them is,
Well, you did something, I know

I really think a teacher know
Just what a student should learn
I don't think they are out here
Just for the salary they earn.

Sometimes the teacher is taking time
Trying to help your child
Because some parent's don't show interest,
And the children just run wild.

Don't put off your children's homework
Just to watch your TV show,
Take time to help that child
With the work that he or she doesn't know

Please take interest in your children
And show them that you care
Don't make them study all alone,
You, too, can their lessons share.

Often stress to them
The importance of education,
For it is very essential for them
To help us and the nation

Maybe you didn't have a chance
To go on and finish high school
But don't hinder your child from finishing,
For we're under another rule

Maybe you didn't have to read or write
To get a job back there,
You just went on working
Hoping to get your share.

You can hardly get a job now
Unless you can read and write.
If you can't fill out the application,
You're turned down because of that plight;

But now there is no excuse now,
For schools are opened at night
To help parent get an education
And not is a parasite.

I think that we parents should strive
To attend the PTA
Take time to meet the teachers
They won't turn you away.

Get acquainted with them
And find out about your boy or girl;
Whether they get their lesson,
Or choose some other joy.

Don't' expect the teacher to do it all,
They have a lot of work;
They have to make out their reports,
So teach your child not to shirk.

Do all you can to help the child,
That will help the teacher too,
Then if the child should fail,
The fault won't be on you.

I have two children in school,
But I surely take time out
And make them study their lesson
Although sometimes they pout.

We'll have to learn to deny ourselves
And put our children first,
If we want them to go forward
And not gradually get worse.

I guess that I've said enough now
But please taken in what I've said.
Don't watch that TV show so much,
Please help your child instead.

GRUMBLING

Stop grumbling so much and be thankful,
Keep a thankful attitude.
You grumble about the water,
You grumble about the food.

You grumble about the Bishop
The Board of Elders, too.
You grumble about the ministers,
Brother Jim and Sister Sue.

You about the pastor and deacons,
The missionary and the mother,
You grumble about the finance committee,
The sisters and the brothers.

You grumble about the choir,
You grumble about Sunday School.
You grumble about the superintendent
And try to change the rules.

You grumble about the teachers,
The ushers and the cooks.
You grumble about how the food tastes,
You grumble about how it looks.

You grumble about evening service,
And most of the time you're not there.
You're sitting at home grumbling
With your feet propped on a chair,

Well, I've said enough about grumbling for now,
But this I must tell,
If you don't stop grumbling so much
You'll grumble your way to hell!

__Think on These Things__

Think on the thing that is honest.
Think on the thing that is true.
Think of a deed of kindness,
And then go out and do.

You'll find that if you think right,
Life will seem much brighter
Try thinking about Jesus Christ
And your load will be much lighter

Think on the thing that is pure,
And the things that make good sense.
Think of how to lift someone up,
And to help him across the fence

Someone, somewhere might be in need,
No matter where you go.
Think of how you can help him,
Or a kind deed to him show.

Think on the lovely things of life,
And be careful of what you say.
Think on the things of good report,
As you go along the way.

Think of the thing that is undefiled,
Not the things that would make someone frown.
Think of how to cheer someone,
Or help someone up who's down.

Most of all,
Think on the Word of God…

Made in the USA
Las Vegas, NV
06 April 2025

20572098R00026